Smart Phonics 1

KB214447

e-future

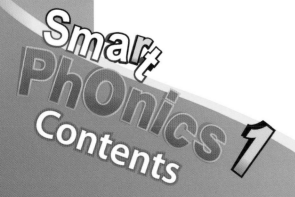

Smart
Phonics
Contents 1

Constant and Cumulative Review

UNIT 4 Jj · Kk · Ll

Step 1

Circle and write.

1. (j) k l
2. G H I
3. j k l
4. G H I
5. j k l
6. J K L
7. G H I
8. J K L
9. j k l

A Write the partner letter.

1. A → a
2. B → ___
3. ___ → c
4. ___ → d
5. ___ → e
6. ___ → f
7. G → ___
8. ___ → H
9. ___ → I
10. ___ → j
11. ___ → k
12. ___ → l

21

Step 2

Circle and match.

1. G — g h i
2. H — g h i
3. I — g h i
4. J — j k l
5. K — j k l
6. L — j k l

Circle the correct pictures.

1. Jj →
2. Kk →
3. Ll →

22

Smart Phonics 1

Step	Cumulative Target Practice	Skills
1	New & Old Targets 1	Reading/Writing
2	New & Old Targets 2	Reading/Writing
3	New & Old Targets 3	Reading/Writing
4	New & Old Targets 4	Writing + Visualization (A)
5	New & Old Targets 5	Writing + Link and Review (B)

is Key to Success in Learning Phonics!

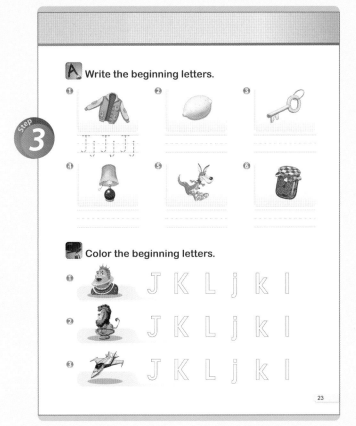

Step 3

A Write the beginning letters.

Color the beginning letters.

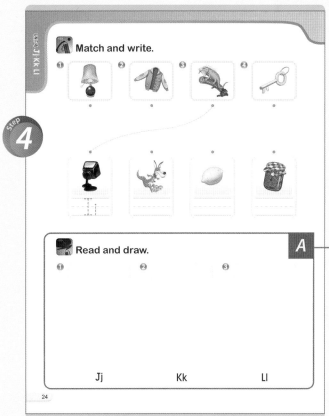

Step 4

UNIT 4 Jj Kk Ll

Match and write.

Read and draw.

①	②	③
Jj	Kk	Ll

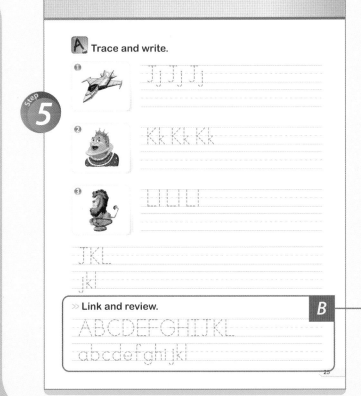

Step 5

A Trace and write.

① Jj Jj Jj

② Kk Kk Kk

③ Ll Ll Ll

J K L

j k l

>> Link and review.   **B**

ABCDEFGHIJKL

abcdefghijkl

Challenge Your Brain!

A Visualization

Children choose the words with the target sounds, visualize the pictures of the words and draw them in the space provided. This activity will help children remember the target words and sounds better.

B Link and Review

Children revisit the old target letters and link them to the new target letters. This activity will help children differentiate capital letters and small letters in sequence.

 **Circle and write.**

①
(Aa) Bb Cc

AaAa

②
Aa Bb Cc

③
Aa Bb Cc

④
Aa Bb Cc

⑤
Aa Bb Cc

⑥
Aa Bb Cc

⑦
Aa Bb Cc

⑧
Aa Bb Cc

⑨
Aa Bb Cc

 **Match.**

1  A • • c •  • •

2 B • • a •  • •

3 C • • b •  • •

 **Circle the correct pictures.**

1  ➡

2  ➡

3  ➡

 Write the beginning letters.

AaAa

 Color the beginning letters.

 A B C a b c

A B C a b c

A B C a b c

8

 **Match and color.**

1  Aa

2  Bb

3  Cc

 **Read and draw.**

1

Aa

2

Aa

3

Bb

4

Cc

 **Trace and write.**

1

Aa Aa Aa

2

Bb Bb Bb

3

Cc Cc Cc

ABC

abc

 **Circle and write.**

1
(Dd) Ee Ff

2
Aa Bb Cc

3
Dd Ee Ff

4
Aa Bb Cc

5
Dd Ee Ff

6
Aa Bb Cc

7
Aa Bb Cc

8
Dd Ee Ff

9
Dd Ee Ff

10
Aa Bb Cc

11
Dd Ee Ff

12
Aa Bb Cc

 **Circle and match.**

① B
a (b) c

② F
d e f

③ E
d e f

④ D
d e f

⑤ C
a b c

⑥ F
d e f

⑦ E
d e f

⑧ D
d e f

 **Write the partner letter.**

① A ⟶ ② B ⟶ ③ C

④ ⟶ d ⑤ ⟶ e ⑥ ⟶ f

 **Circle the correct picture.**

①  **Dd** →

②  **Ee** →

③  **Ff** →

 **Color the beginning letters.**

①  D E F d e f

②  D E F d e f

③  D E F d e f

 **Match and write.**

①   → _____

②   → _____

③   →

 **Read and draw.**

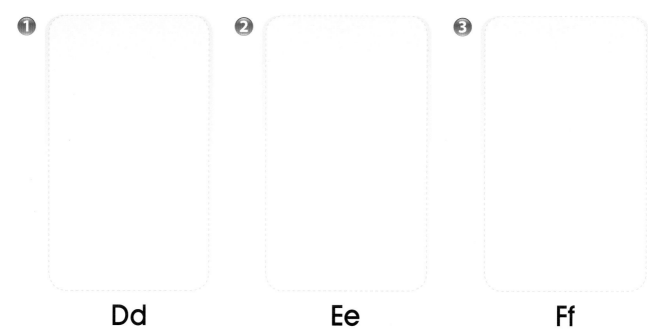

①   ②   ③

Dd   Ee   Ff

 **Trace and write.**

Dd Dd Dd

Ee Ee Ee

Ff Ff Ff

DEF

def

>> **Link and review.**

ABCDEF

abcdef

  **Circle and write.**

①  (Gg) Hh Ii

G̣g̣ G̣g̣

②  Dd Ee Ff

③  Aa Bb Cc

④  Gg Hh Ii

⑤  Gg Hh Ii

⑥  Aa Bb Cc

⑦ 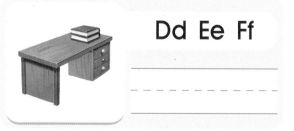 Dd Ee Ff

⑧  Gg Hh Ii

⑨  Dd Ee Ff

⑩ 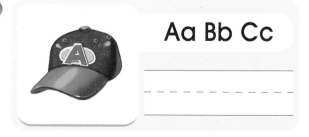 Aa Bb Cc

 Circle the correct beginning letter.

① (g) h

② H I

③ f h

④ C D

⑤ h i

⑥ G H

⑦ h i

⑧ A E

 Circle the correct picture.

① Gg →

② Hh →

③ Ii →

 **Color the beginning letters.**

① D E F d e f

② G H I g h i

③ A B C a b c

④ G H I g h i

⑤ A B C a b c

⑥ G H I g h i

⑦ D E F d e f

 **Write the beginning letters.**

①

$C\ c\quad C\ c$

②

③

④

⑤

⑥

 **Read and draw.**

①

②

③

Gg

Hh

Ii

 **Trace and write.**

①

Gg Gg Gg

②

Hh Hh Hh

③

Ii Ii Ii

GHI

ghi

>> **Link and review.**

ABCDEFGHI

abcdefghi

 Circle and write.

① j k l

② G H I

③ j k l

④ G H I

⑤ j k l

⑥ J K L

⑦ G H I

⑧ J K L

⑨ j k l

A Write the partner letter.

① A a → ② B → ③ c → ④ d

⑤ e → ⑥ f → ⑦ G → ⑧ H

⑨ I → ⑩ j → ⑪ k → ⑫ l

UNIT 4 Jj·Kk·Ll

 **Circle and match.**

① G
 (g) h i

② H
g h i

③ I
g h i

④ J
j k l

⑤ K
j k l

⑥ L
j k l

 **Circle the correct pictures.**

① Jj →

② Kk →

③ Ll →

22

 # Write the beginning letters.

①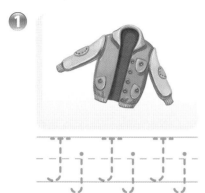

J j J j J j

②

③

④

⑤

⑥

 # Color the beginning letters.

①

J K L j k l

②

J K L j k l

③

J K L j k l

 **Match and write.**

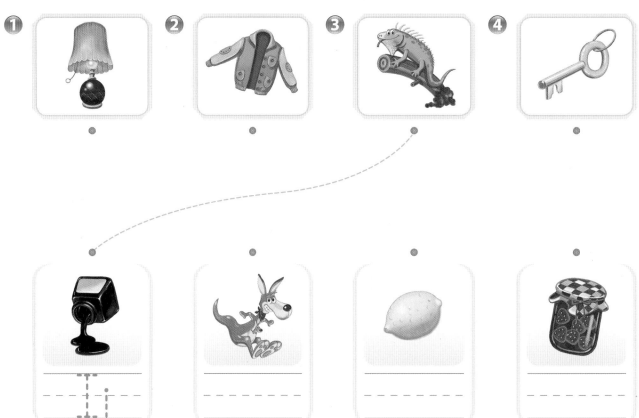

 **Read and draw.**

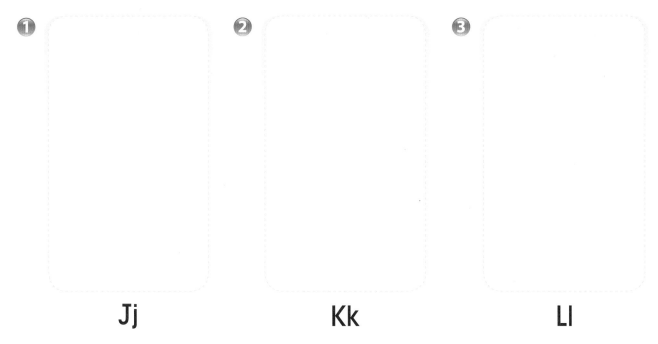

Jj   Kk   Ll

 Trace and write.

J j J j J j

Kk Kk Kk

L l L l L l

J K L

j k l

» Link and review.

A B C D E F G H I J K L

a b c d e f g h i j k l

 **Match and write.**

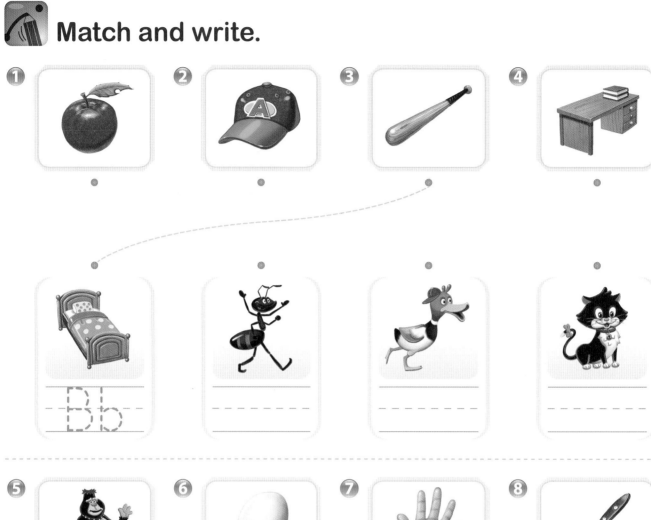

Bb

 **Match.**

①  **Ii**

②  **Jj**

③ **Kk**

④ **Ll**

 **Circle the correct beginning letter.**

①

c   k

②

f   g

③

a   e

④

b   h

⑤

B   D

⑥

b   d

⑦

I   G

⑧

A   E

 **Write the beginning letters.**

①

E e E e E e

②

③

④

⑤

⑥

⑦

⑧

⑨

⑩

⑪

⑫

 # Circle the correct picture.

① Aa

② Bb

③ Cc

④ Dd

⑤ Ee

⑥ Ff

⑦ Gg

⑧ Hh

 **Choose and write.**

①
Gg

②
Hh

③
Ii

①

②

③

④

⑤

⑥

⑦

⑧

⑨

⑩

⑪

⑫

④
Jj

⑤
Kk

⑥
Ll

UNIT 5 Mm · Nn · Oo

 **Circle the correct beginning letter.**

①  J (K) L

②  M N O

③  m n o

④  j k l

⑤  m n o

⑥  M N O

⑦  m n o

⑧  M N O

 **Write the partner letter.**

① D d → ② E ☐ → ③ ☐ f → ④ ☐ g

→ ⑤ ☐ h → ⑥ ☐ i → ⑦ J ☐ → ⑧ K ☐

→ ⑨ L ☐ → ⑩ ☐ m → ⑪ ☐ n → ⑫ ☐ o

 **Match.**

①

②

③

④

(h) (I) (j) (K) (l) (M) (n) (O)

⑤

⑥

⑦

⑧

 **Circle the correct picture.**

① **Mm** →

② **Nn** →

③ **Oo** →

 **Match and write.**

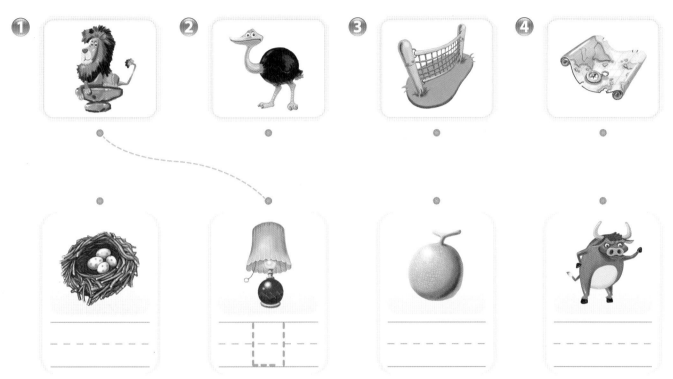

 **Color the beginning letters.**

① M N O m n o

② M N O m n o

③ M N O m n o

 **Write the beginning letters.**

①

G g G g

②

③

④

⑤

⑥

 **Read and draw.**

① ② ③

Mm   Nn   Oo

 **Trace and write.**

①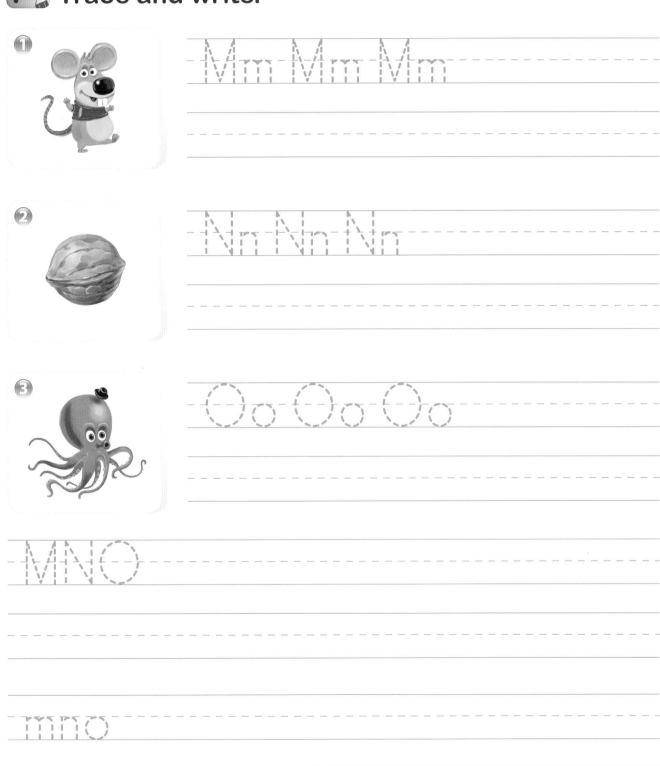

Mm Mm Mm

② Nn Nn Nn

③ Oo Oo Oo

MNO

mno

 **Circle and write.**

1

(Pp) Qq Rr

2

Pp Qq Rr

3

Jj Kk Ll

4

Jj Kk Ll

5

Pp Qq Rr

6

Mm Nn Oo

7

Jj Kk Ll

8

Pp Qq Rr

9

Pp Qq Rr

10

Mm Nn Oo

11

Pp Qq Rr

12

Mm Nn Oo

 **Match.**

1 Kk

2 Ll

3 Mm

4 Nn

5 Oo

6 Pp

7 Qq

8 Rr

 **Circle the correct picture.**

1 Pp →

2 Qq →

3 Rr →

 Write the beginning letters.

Mm Mm

 Color the beginning letters.

P Q R p q r

P Q R p q r

P Q R p q r

 **Match and write.**

 **Read and draw.**

Pp   Qq   Rr

 **Trace and write.**

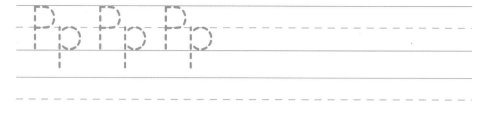

PQR

pqr

>> **Link and review.**

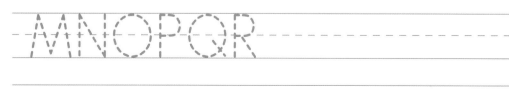

 **Write the beginning letter.**

① S s

② t

③ V

④ u

⑤ t

⑥ V

⑦ S

⑧ u

Match.

①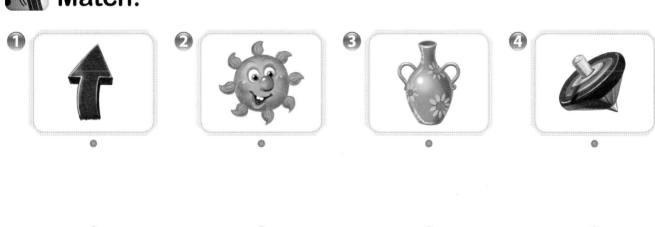

②

③

④

 **Circle the correct picture.**

①

Pp

②

Qq

③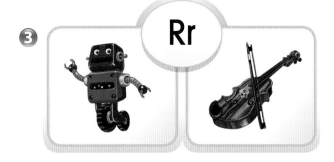

Rr

④

Ss

 **Color the beginning letters.**

①  S T U V s t u v

②  S T U V s t u v

③  S T U V s t u v

④  S T U V s t u v

 **Circle the correct beginning letter.**

① m n

② c k

③ l r

④ u o

⑤ p q

⑥ j i

⑦ u o

⑧ u v

 **Write the partner letter.**

① K k ➡

② L _____ ➡

③ _____ m ➡

④ _____ n

⑤ ➡ _____ o ➡

⑥ _____ p ➡

⑦ Q _____ ➡

⑧ R _____

⑨ ➡ S _____ ➡

⑩ _____ t ➡

⑪ _____ u ➡

⑫ _____ v

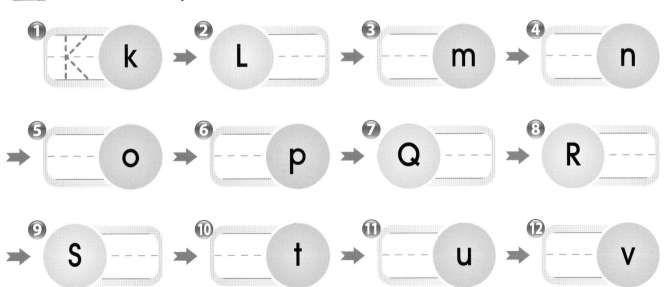

 **Match and write.**

①  ②  ③  ④

Ss

 **Read and draw.**

① Ss

② Tt

③ Uu

④ Vv

 **Trace and write.**

Ss Ss

Tt Tt

Uu Uu

Vv Vv

STUV

stuv

>> **Link and review.**

MNOPQRSTUV

mnopqrstuv

 Circle the correct beginning or ending letter.

1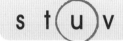
s t (u) v

2
s t u v

3
w x y z

4
s t u v

5
S T U V

6
W X Y Z

7
W X Y Z

8
S T U V

9
w x y z

10
u v w x

11
w x y z

12
s t u v

13
W X Y Z

14
W X Y Z

15
S T U V

16
W X Y Z

 **Circle and match.**

1. u
   T (U) V

2. v
   T U V

3. W
   w x y

4. X
   w x y

5. Y
   w x y

6. Z
   x y z

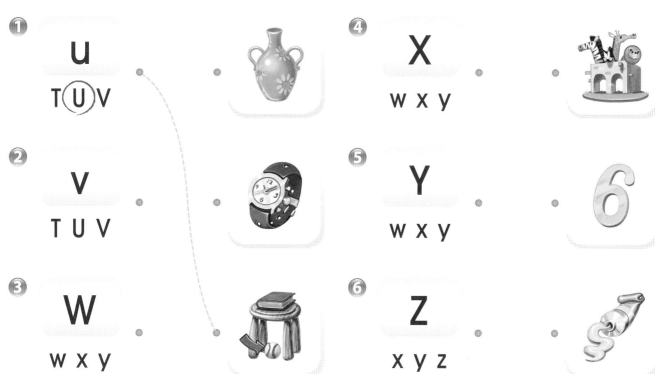

 **Circle the correct picture.**

1. Ww

2. Xx

3. Yy

4. Zz

 **Match and write.**

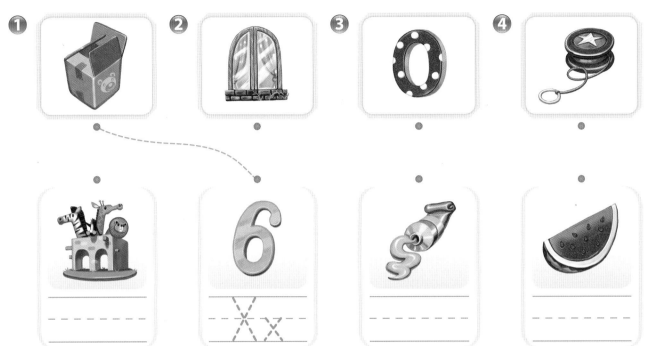

 **Color the beginning or ending letters.**

A Write the beginning or ending letters.

① ② ③

④ ⑤ ⑥

 Read and draw.

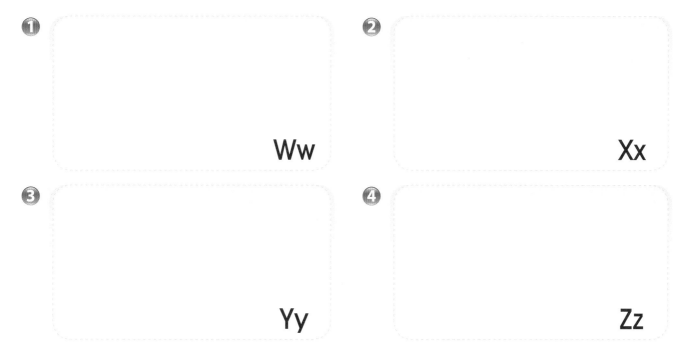

① Ww ② Xx

③ Yy ④ Zz

 **Trace and write.**

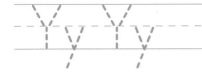

>> **Link and review.**

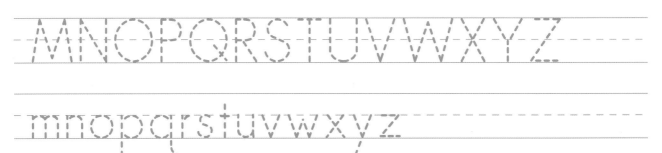

A Choose and write.

① m	② n	③ o	④ p	⑤ q	⑥ r	⑦ s

① ② ③ ④

⑤ ⑥ ⑦

⑧ ⑨ ⑩ ⑪

⑫ ⑬ ⑭

⑧ t	⑨ u	⑩ v	⑪ w	⑫ x	⑬ y	⑭ z

  # Write the beginning letters.

①

S_s S_s

②

③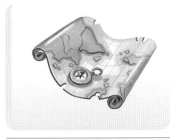

④

⑤

⑥

⑦

⑧

⑨

⑩

⑪

⑫

 Circle the correct picture.

① Mm

② Nn

③ Oo

④ Pp

 Write the partner letter.

① M → ② ___ n → ③ O ___ → ④ ___ p

→ ⑤ Q ___ → ⑥ ___ r → ⑦ S ___ →

⑧ T ___ → ⑨ ___ u → ⑩ V ___ → ⑪ ___ w

→ ⑫ X ___ → ⑬ ___ y → ⑭ Z ___

 # Circle the correct beginning letter.

①

M N O

②

U V W

③

M N O

④

S T U

⑤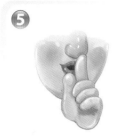

O Q R

⑥

X Y Z

⑦

W X Y

⑧

X Y Z

⑨

s t u

⑩

m n o

⑪

u v w

⑫

p q r

⑬

w y z

⑭

p q r

⑮

u v w

⑯

x y z

 **Match.**

1. Oo

2. Pp

3. Qq

4. Rr

5. Ss

6. Tt

7. Uu

8. Vv

9. Ww

10. Xx

11. Yy

12. Zz

CHALLENGE Aa~Zz

 Circle the correct beginning letter.

1

b   d

2

m   n

3

g   h

4

b   d

5

h   y

6

a   e

7

l   r

8

a   e

9

m   n

10

i   j

11

c   k

12

p   q

13

o   u

14

i   j

15

f   p

16

c   k

 **Match.**

1 T · · q ·  ·

2 Q · · r ·  ·

3 U · · t ·  ·

4 R · · s ·  ·

5 V · · u ·  ·

6 S · · v ·  ·

 **Write the partner letter.**

A a → b → C

→ d → E → f

→ G → H → i

→ J → k → L

→ m → N → O

→ p → Q → R

→ s → T → U

→ v → W → X

→ y → Z

 # Circle the correct picture.

1. **Dd**
2. **Ff**
3. **Gg**
4. **Ii**
5. **Ww**
6. **Xx**
7. **Yy**
8. **Zz**

Smart
Phonics